A Day at the RACES

W9-CBJ-413

by Eric Michaels
Illustrated by Elizabeth Wolf

MODERN CURRICULUM PRESS

Modern Curriculum Press
An Imprint of Pearson Learning
299 Jefferson Road, P.O. Box 480
Parsippany, NJ 07054–0480

Internet address:
http://www.pearsonlearning.com

© 1999 Modern Curriculum Press. All rights reserved. Printed in the United States of America. This publication, or parts thereof, may not be reproduced in any form by photographic, electronic, mechanical, or any other method, for any use, including information storage and retrieval, without written permission from the publisher. This edition is published simultaneously in Canada by Pearson Education Canada.

Design by Design 5 and Agatha Jaspon

ISBN: 0–7652–0883–0

3 4 5 6 7 8 9 10 MA 05 04 03 02 01 00

Contents

Chapter 1

Goodbye, Fall Fling

"It looks like there will be no Fall Fling this year," Mindy said to her twin brother, Mack, and her friends, Jessie and Luis.

It was the end of the summer. School was going to start next week right after the Labor Day weekend.

"What? That's the best day of the year! Everyone in Morganville is looking forward to the Fall Fling," moaned Luis.

"People have been in training all summer," Jessie said.

"My mom probably will be the most disappointed person of all," Jessie added. "She was supposed to be in charge of the Fall Fling this year. She's already asked Mayor Diaz to be one of the judges. She also has some great ideas for raising even more money than last year for the community center kitchen."

"Our dad was sure he would beat Mr. Chen in the one-mile run this year," Mack said.

"Why did Mrs. Cranberry have to move to Florida and sell Dellwood Farm, anyway?" grumbled Luis. "She always let us have the Fall Fling on the big field behind her house."

"My mom spoke to the new owners of Dellwood Farm," Jessie said. "They've turned the farm back into a real farm. They don't want anyone tramping on the crops."

Mack twirled a strand of red hair around his finger. He looked thoughtful. Mindy knew that look very well. It meant his brain was working too hard.

"I've got it!" he said. "We'll ask Mom and Dad if we can have the Fall Fling in our backyard."

"Mack Singer, you're an impossible brother!" Mindy said. "Our backyard wasn't big enough to have everyone in our family for the summer barbecue. Where would we run a three-mile race?"

Jessie, Luis, and Mack sat on the steps of the front porch looking glum.

"It looks like the end of a great tradition," said Jessie.

"I don't know about you guys, but I will not give up," Mindy said.

Chapter 2

A Girl Named Amanda Singleton

Mack and Mindy talked about the Fall Fling during most of Labor Day weekend. They couldn't think of any way to get the new owners of Dellwood Farm to let the town use their big field for the Fall Fling.

Before they knew it, the last weekend of summer was over.

"Where is my lucky four-leaf clover key chain?" called Mack on the first day of school. "I can't go to school without it!"

"Mack, you're impossible! Your key chain is hooked onto your backpack where you put it last night," Mindy called back.

"Mack, Mindy, where are you?" called their mom. "The school bus will be here in five minutes."

Mindy was moving slower than usual. She liked school, and the beginning of school meant that it wouldn't be long before the Fall Fling. Only this year, at the end of September, there wasn't going to be a Fall Fling.

Mindy gasped when she looked at the clock. Both she and Mack had to rush for the bus. They made it just in time.

When Mindy got to her classroom, she looked around to see who was in her class. Morganville was not a very big place, so she thought she would know everyone.

She began to daydream as her new teacher, Mr. Clayton, took attendance.

"Jessie Rogers."
"Here," said Jessie.
"Mindy Singer."
"Here," Mindy said.
"Amanda Singleton."
"Here," said a girl in the front row.

Just then Mr. Clayton looked up from the list of names.

"By the way, I'd like everyone to meet Amanda Singleton," he said. "She is new to Morganville. Her family lives on Dellwood Farm."

"DELLWOOD FARM!" Mindy said out loud.

Everyone turned to stare at her. She didn't care. If she could talk to Amanda, there still might be a way to have the Fall Fling!

Chapter 3

A Problem at Dellwood Farm

At lunchtime, Mindy and Jessie looked for Mack and Luis. They all sat together at a table.

"You'll never guess who's in our class," Mindy began.

"Who?" asked Mack.

"A new girl named Amanda Singleton," she replied.

"Guess where Amanda Singleton lives," said Jessie, who was beginning to catch on.

"DELLWOOD FARM!" Mindy shouted.

Just then Mindy saw Amanda holding a lunch tray. She was standing near their table.

Mindy jumped up and called, "Hey, Amanda, come on and sit with us."

Amanda came over and sat down.

"Hi," she said shyly.

Mindy quickly introduced Amanda to her brother and Luis.

"Hey, Amanda," said Mack. "How come your parents won't let us have the Fall Fling at Dellwood Farm?"

"What Fall Fling?" Amanda asked with a puzzled look. "I don't know what you're talking about."

Everyone took turns telling Amanda all about the Fall Fling. They talked about the games and the food. They even mentioned the money the Fling raised for the community center kitchen. Jessie told Amanda that her mom had even spoken to Amanda's parents about it.

"Mom and Dad never said anything to me about it," said Amanda. "My parents are trying to turn Dellwood Farm back into a real farm," she added.

"We know, we know," said Jessie. "That's what my mom said after she talked to your parents."

"We've got lots of crops," said Amanda proudly. "We'll be ready to harvest most of them by the end of this month."

Just then her smile turned into a frown.

"What's the matter, Amanda?" Mindy asked.

"You know that field in back of my house?" she said.

Everyone nodded. The field in back of Amanda's house was all they had been thinking about all summer.

"My mom and I planted some corn and lots of vegetables in that field," Amanda explained. "We wanted to open a vegetable stand. Everything will be ready to harvest in a few weeks along with the other crops. But my dad hasn't been able to hire all the people he needs to help with harvesting. So, he says whatever we can pick by hand is all that we can get from that field for the stand."

"All of our hard work will be for nothing if we can't pick all those vegetables," Amanda said, sadly.

Suddenly, Mindy had an idea.

"Do you think your parents would let us have the Fall Fling if we helped to harvest the crops in that field?" she asked.

"What do you mean?" asked Amanda.

Mindy explained her idea to Amanda, Mack, Luis, and Jessie. They all thought it sounded good.

Chapter 4

Plans Are Made

After school, Mack and Mindy ran all the way home from the bus stop. They were in a hurry to tell their parents about Amanda Singleton and the plan for having the Fall Fling after all.

"If we help Amanda and her mom harvest their vegetables, we might be able to have the Fall Fling," Mack said excitedly at dinner that evening.

"It's not that simple," said Mrs. Singer. "First of all, that field is pretty big. It will take more people than you two, Jessie, Luis, and Amanda to harvest it all."

"I don't think the Singletons would want people running all over their field anyway," said their dad.

Mack and Mindy felt all their excitement drain away.

Later that evening, Mindy spoke to Jessie.

"Did you speak to your mom about our idea for having the Fall Fling?" she asked.

"Yes," Jessie sighed. "She still didn't think it would work."

"Neither did mine," Mindy said. "Wait a minute!" She suddenly had another idea. "What if we changed the Fall Fling so that the races were harvesting races?"

"What are you talking about, Mindy? What are harvesting races?" asked Jessie.

"You know," Mindy said. "We could have the kind of relay races we have at school in the gym. We can have different kinds of races to harvest the different kinds of vegetables," she went on.

"Mindy," Jessie said happily, "you're crazy! But maybe it will work."

Chapter 5

Let the Fling Begin!

Believe it or not, Amanda's parents agreed to let the town use their field for the Fall Fling as long as the races would be harvest races and not running races. The whole town of Morganville was excited.

The racers kept right on training. They practiced running and bending and carrying. They talked about the best way to pick a cucumber or a bean from a vine.

Everyone was on some kind of planning committee. No one could stop talking about the new Fall Fling.

Finally the day of the Fall Fling arrived. Mr. Singer woke everyone early. He was cooking breakfast.

"Come on, sleepyheads," he said. "You need energy for the races. And I need my lucky running shorts. Who has seen them?" He went into the laundry room, looking for his shorts while their dog, Digger, barked at him.

Mrs. Singer called out to him, "Try the top drawer of the dresser."

Mack and Mindy filed into the kitchen.

"Hurry," she said. "We need to get going."

Mack and Mindy ran to the van. Digger jumped in behind them while Mrs. Singer honked for Mr. Singer.

He came out of the house wearing a pair of bright red shorts. They had cartoon mice running up and down the legs.

Mindy tried not to laugh. "What happened to your lucky shorts?" she asked.

Mr. Singer frowned and shrugged.

"I think Dad looks very . . . um, nice," Mrs. Singer said.

"Sorry, kids," Mr. Singer said as he got in the van. "I don't have any more time to look for my lucky shorts. And these are the only other pair of running shorts I have. Besides, we should be thinking about the Fall Fling. Did I tell you how to pick a tomato without crushing it?"

Mindy looked at Mack. He was rolling his eyes.

Digger barked as the van moved. They were off to the Fall Fling!

Chapter 6

Bean Pickers

When they got to Dellwood Farm, Amanda's parents and the food committee were putting up long tables in the yard behind the house. People were bringing food from their cars. Baskets, small boxes, and large wooden bins were stacked at one end of the field.

Mindy saw Mr. Clayton, her teacher, and Mr. Chen, who always beat her dad in the one-mile race. He was wearing brand-new running clothes.

"Nice shorts," Mr. Clayton yelled to Mr. Singer.

Mr. Singer frowned.

There were lots of people Mindy didn't know, too. Some tourists always came to town to see the Fall Fling. But this year there were more. Mindy guessed they had heard about the harvest races.

Finally, she spotted Jessie and Luis with Mack. They ran over.

"Can you believe this crowd?" Luis said.

Mindy's mom hurried over to give Jessie's mother the starting whistle. She took it and blew hard. Everyone stopped talking.

"Attention," she called. "We're here to get the field harvested and have some fun. So everyone gather around here and listen."

She said, "These aren't just speed races. We need to get lots of vegetables out of the field today and in one piece! The Singletons are giving some of everything we pick to the community center kitchen. The rest will go to their vegetable stand."

Everyone cheered.

Mayor Diaz was in charge of announcing the races. She was trying to explain the first race to the contestants. Every time she moved or spoke, the big floppy hat she was wearing flopped over in her face. The racers watched her in confusion.

"Will the bean pickers please come forward," she bellowed. Five people, one for each row of bean plants, came forward. One of them was Mrs. Singer. Next to her stood her friend Mrs. Rose, talking as usual. Each racer was given a basket.

"Whoever picks the most beans in 10 minutes wins the race," Mayor Diaz went on. "When you fill one basket, come back and get another one! So, is everybody ready?"

Jessie's mom yelled, "On your mark, get set, GO!" She blew her whistle.

The racers ran forward, plopped their baskets at the beginning of the bean rows, and began to pick. Mrs. Singer's fingers were picking so fast, they looked like a blur. Mrs. Rose was busy talking to Mr. Rodelli in the next row. She kept dropping her beans.

It seemed only a minute before Mrs. Singer was carrying her full basket back to the end of the row.

Mindy cheered, "Go, Mom!"

Ms. Carson, the gym teacher, ran up with her second full basket just before Mrs. Singer brought hers. It was a close race.

Jessie's mom was getting ready to blow the whistle for the end of the race. Mrs. Singer finished her third basket. Ms. Carson finished hers at the same time. They raced together to the end of the row. Ms. Carson put her basket down just a second before Mindy's mom did. Then the whistle blew.

Mack and Mindy rushed over to their mom. She was breathing hard, but she was smiling.

Mack patted her on the back. "You came in second! That's great!"

"Not bad for a mom, huh?" she asked.

"Not bad at all," Mindy said.

"We've got to go," Mrs. Singer said. "Your dad is in the pumpkin race."

Chapter 7

Pumpkin Rollers

"Attention, everyone! It's time for the pumpkin race," yelled Mayor Diaz.

"Dad, you're on!" Mindy called out.

Mr. Singer ran over. He frowned and looked down at his shorts.

"Maybe I won't race," he said.

"Come on!" Mrs. Singer said. "If I can do it, so can you."

Four people lined up. Mr. Chen stood next to Mr. Singer.

"There will be a prize for the person who picks the largest pumpkin," said Mayor Diaz. "There will also be a prize for the person who picks the most pumpkins."

Mr. Singer looked down at Mr. Chen's feet. "New shoes?" he smiled.

"New shorts?" Mr. Chen smiled back.

Before Mindy's dad could say anything, Jessie's mom blew the starting whistle.

Mr. Chen took the lead right away. Mr. Singer was close behind. Mindy could see her dad staring at Mr. Chen's shoes. He looked down at the mice on his shorts. Then he stumbled over a pumpkin and almost fell.

All of the racers grabbed their first pumpkins. Holding them carefully, they ran back to the edge of the field. Everyone watching the race was jumping up and down and cheering.

Mr. Singer saw he was falling behind. He tried to pick up two pumpkins, but one kept sliding to the ground. Finally, he was able to get both pumpkins into his arms.

He started to run. Just before he reached the edge of the field, he dropped one of the pumpkins. It landed with a plop and broke into several pieces.

"At least you got one, Dad!" Mindy called to him. He smiled tiredly.

"Go for the big one, Dad!" Mack yelled. His dad tried to see where Mack was pointing. There, far down the field, was the biggest pumpkin Mack and Mindy had ever seen.

Their dad saw it at the same time as Mr. Chen. The mice on his shorts were a blur as he ran as fast as he could to the pumpkin. He beat Mr. Chen by a few seconds.

"What is he going to do?" Mindy said to Mack. "He can't pick it up. It's too heavy."

"He's going to roll it," Mack pointed out.

Mack was right. His dad was trying to push the pumpkin over on its side. Finally, the pumpkin tipped onto its side. Then he started pushing.

The pumpkin moved slowly at first. Then it picked up speed. Soon, Mr. Singer was chasing it down the field. Everyone had to get out of the way as he crossed the finish line behind his giant rolling pumpkin.

"Mr. Chen wins the prize for the most pumpkins picked," Mayor Diaz announced. Mr. Chen waved to the crowd.

"And for the biggest pumpkin, the prize goes to Mr. Singer," she said.

Mack and Mindy jumped up and down and cheered wildly. Their dad didn't need his lucky shorts after all.

Chapter 8

Crushed Tomatoes

"The tomato relay is next," Mayor Diaz said.

"That's your race," Mrs. Singer said to Mack and Mindy.

"I've got to get Jessie and Luis, too," Mindy said. "We're a team for this race."

She dashed off and found them over by the food tables. They hurried back and lined up to listen to the rules.

"One person on each team will be the tomato picker," Jessie's mom explained. "The tomato picker will give each tomato to the second person on the team. The second person gives the tomato to the third person. The third person gives it to the fourth person who puts the tomato into the team's box. You have to be careful."

Mack, Jessie, Luis, and Mindy spread out to form a line. They could hear the shouts and cheers from the crowd.

Jessie's mom blew the starting whistle.

Mack pulled a tomato off the vine. He ran to where Mindy was waiting and threw it into her hand. The tomato broke.

"Mack!" Mindy said. "You have to be careful! Just hand it to me."

"I'm sorry," he said, running back for another one. This time he put the tomato gently into her hand. She passed it to Luis. Luis passed it to Jessie, who put it in the box. The minute Jessie put it in the box, Mack had another tomato off the plant. The children started passing them faster and faster.

"Let's go," Jessie yelled. "Our box is almost full."

Luis tossed the tomato he was holding like a baseball. In his excitement, he forgot he was holding a tomato.

The Singers' dog, Digger, had been watching the race. Digger must have thought Luis was throwing a ball, too.

Digger jumped high to get it, twisting in the air. When he came down, the tomato was in his mouth.

"Digger!" cried Mrs. Singer. "Come here!"

The children kept picking and passing tomatoes until Jessie yelled, "That's it. The box is full!"

They all took a deep breath as the judges looked over each team's box. They picked out any tomatoes that were cracked or bruised.

Then Mayor Diaz announced, "Mack, Mindy, Luis, and Jessie win the tomato race!"

They could not believe it. All the parents started cheering.

Chapter 9

Corn Pickers

After the tomato race, Mindy found Amanda Singleton taking pictures with her camera.

"Put your camera down," Mindy said. "I signed us up to be partners in the corn-picking race."

They ran over to the rows of corn and grabbed a basket.

"This race is just like the bean race," Mayor Diaz said. "The winning team is the one who can fill the most baskets with corn. So get those baskets ready."

When the whistle blew, Amanda and Mindy ran to the first row. Amanda started to pick the ears toward the top. Mindy began at the bottom.

Just then, Jimmy, Jessie's little brother, came racing through the stalks. Digger was close behind. He and Digger bumped into Amanda and Mindy. They all fell in a heap with the cornstalk on top of them. Everyone giggled. Digger barked.

After they had filled their basket, Amanda and Mindy each took a handle and lifted it. They started off down the row.

"Wait a minute," Amanda said. "Are we going the right way?"

"I don't know," Mindy replied, looking up and down the row. "The corn is too big to see over."

"This is like a maze," said Amanda. "How do we get out of here?"

"Listen!" Mindy said. She could hear Digger barking. "Let's follow Digger's barking."

They finally ended up on the other side of the field. By the time they got their basket back to the finish line, all the other teams were done. They watched as the winners got their prize, a case of popcorn.

"I'm glad we didn't win," Amanda said. "I'm tired of corn by now."

"Was that the last race?" Mindy asked.

"I think my parents have one more event they want to do," Amanda replied.

Chapter 10

The Final Event

By now, all the racers were tired and hot. Everyone took a break to drink lemonade and have some food. As they were eating, Amanda's parents came up to thank everyone for helping.

"Because of your help," Mrs. Singleton said, "we were able to harvest almost the whole field."

"Don't worry about the Fall Fling next year," Mr. Singleton added. "We're going to make Dellwood Farm the official Fall Fling headquarters."

Everyone cheered for the Singletons.

"As a way to say thanks," Mr. Singleton said, "we've set up one final event. We're going to have a scarecrow-dressing contest."

"What's that?" Mindy asked.

"Teams will each dress a scarecrow. The best-looking and funniest-looking scarecrows win a prize," Mrs. Singleton explained.

"Come on, Mom," Mindy said. "Let's be a team with Amanda and Jessie."

Everyone rushed over to where the Singletons had set up five T-shaped poles for scarecrows. They had stuffed pillowcases with straw and put them on top of the poles for heads. They had also put out a couple of big boxes filled with old clothes.

When the whistle blew, the teams ran over to one of the boxes. Jessie and Mindy started digging through the clothes. Shirts, pants, scarves, and hats flew everywhere.

They hurried over and gave Amanda and Mrs. Singer what they had found. Everyone started dressing the scarecrow.

They put a big, ragged shirt on the pole first. Over this they put a vest with big red flowers on it. Then Mrs. Singer put a plaid tie around its neck. Finally, Mindy stuck a baseball cap on its head.

"There's something missing," she said.

"I know," Amanda said. "Our scarecrow has no pants."

They went back to the boxes to look. There were no pants, shorts, or anything left!

Suddenly, Mindy heard growling from her family's van. Digger was pulling on something under the seat. With a tearing sound, whatever it was came loose. Then Digger ran toward them.

"What's that in his mouth?" Mrs. Singer asked.

As Digger ran up, wagging his tail, Mindy saw what he had in his mouth. It was her dad's lucky shorts. They must have been under the back seat of the van all this time. And now they had a big hole in them.

Mrs. Singer started to giggle. "Well, they're better than nothing," she said. She quickly put them on the scarecrow.

Just as the judges got to their scarecrow, Mr. Singer came over to take a closer look.

He shouted, "Those are my lucky shorts!"

Mindy asked her dad please not to say
anything. The judges ended up giving them
the prize for the funniest scarecrow.

"I'm glad those shorts were lucky for
somebody," Mr. Singer said.

On the way home, Mindy looked at the
ribbons she had won at the Fall Fling. She
smiled to herself and said, "This was the best
Fall Fling ever! I can't wait until next year!"

Glossary

attention (uh TEN shun) the act of watching something carefully

committee (kuh MIHT ee) a small group of people who work together on something

contestants (kahn TES tuhnts) two or more people who take part in a race or a game

disappointed (dihs uh POINT ed) to be unhappy about not getting something wanted or expected

glum (gluhm) quiet in a gloomy way

harvest (HAHR vest) picking a crop when it is ready to be eaten or used

hire (hyr) to agree to pay someone money to work

maze (mayz) a series of passages or paths that may be bordered by high bushes or plants so it is hard to find a way out

scarecrow (SKAIR kroh) a made-up figure of a person put in a field of crops to scare the birds away

tradition (trah DIHSH uhn) a way of doing something that has been handed down by people who lived before and is repeated each year